Old Test~~~~
Prophecy Today

John Goldingay

David Allan Hubbard Professor of Old Testament
Fuller Theological Seminary, Pasadena, California

GROVE BOOKS LIMITED
RIDLEY HALL RD   CAMBRIDGE   CB3 9HU

Contents

This booklet is a slight expansion and revision of a paper that appeared in *The Spirit & Church* 3 (2001) pp 27–46. I have sought to translate it back into British English, but I may not have succeeded. I am grateful to students and faculty colleagues at Fuller Theological Seminary for discussion that contributed to and clarified the paper.

The Cover Illustration is by Peter Ashton

First Impression July 2003
ISSN 1470-8531
ISBN 1 85174 536 X

Introduction

1

Defining prophecy is a notoriously difficult matter.

Any description of prophecy that has bite will turn out not to apply to every Old Testament prophet, let alone to prophets in the New Testament. A definition that does apply to every prophet will turn out to be somewhat vacuous and/or to apply to people other than prophets.

When we cannot define something, or find that our attempts to do so become vacuous, then one strategy is to utilize Ludwig Wittgenstein's notion of 'family resemblances.'[1] A family may have a characteristic profile—a shape of nose and chin, a shape of body, a level of intelligence, a way of walking or thinking, a strength in certain emotions and a weakness in others. Individual members of the family may not have all these characteristics, but to qualify as sharing the family resemblance, they will manifest most of them. In a parallel way, we might suggest that prophets have a set of family resemblances. Individual prophets may then lack some of these without this imperilling their being identified as prophets or imperilling the accuracy of the profile. Conversely, features of character or ministry that appear in only one or two prophets may not be indications of the nature of prophecy but rather may be features of these individuals' ministry or person.

Individual prophets may lack some of these resemblances without this imperilling their being identified as prophets

Another way to make the point would be to consider how prophets differ from other people through whom God may speak and act. In the Old Testament these would include leaders ('judges'), kings, priests, and scholars (the 'wise' of Proverbs). In the New Testament, prophets appear in a list that also includes pastors, teachers, apostles, and evangelists (see Eph 4). The term 'prophecy' itself appears in a list that also includes utterance of knowledge, utterance of wisdom, faith, gifts of healing, working of miracles, discernment of spirits, tongues, and interpretation of tongues (1 Cor 12). The complication in connection with the New Testament is that we are quite unsure of the meaning of many of these terms. In the modern church, we might ask how prophets differ from priests, pastors, worship leaders, education ministers, teachers, counsellors, spiritual directors, and youth ministers—let alone social activists.

The way I will therefore proceed in this booklet is by drawing up a family profile for the Old Testament prophets and comment on the possible contemporary significance of each of the elements.

I make the assumption that we might reasonably expect prophetic ministry to be exercised in the contemporary church. I assume that there is no basis for the claim that the exercise of prophetic ministry was confined to the biblical period. Indeed, that seems to be in conflict with God's promise that the exercise of prophecy will be a feature of the full life that God intends for the chosen people (see Joel 2.28–29).

Questions for Reflection

- In what ways have you experienced the prophetic in your life, ministry or church?

- What was it that made you think these experiences involved the prophetic?

- Where have you gained your understanding of what it means to be prophetic? What place has study of the Old Testament prophets had in this learning?

Nightmares and Dreams

2

A prophet shares God's nightmares and dreams.

Prophets are mediators between heaven and earth. They bring human beings a *word* from God that they could not have attained by ordinary means, or they bring home this word with a distinctive sharpness. And they bring a *vision* from God. The beginning of Isaiah 1 describes what follows as a 'vision'; the beginning of Isaiah 2 describes it as a 'word.'

One of the Old Testament words for a prophet is 'seer' (for example 2 Kgs 17.13). Strictly there are two words, *hozeh* and *ro'eh*, but both are participles from verbs meaning 'see' and they thus correspond well to the English word. Prophets are people who see things that other people cannot see. These may be realities of the present but unseen world (see 1 Kgs 22.15–23; 2 Kgs 2.9–14; 6.15–23). Or they may be realities of the visible but still future world (see for example the man of God in 1 Kgs 13.1–3).

> *Prophets are people who see things that other people cannot see*

Prophets such as Amos, Hosea, Isaiah, and Micah declared that political calamity was coming for the people of God, in large part because of what was wrong in their society. This might seem to suggest that they were either social reformers or astute political commentators or both. As social reformers perhaps they looked at the life of the people of God and perceived an absence of commitment to God and commitment to other members of the community, and they inferred—or were assured by God—that trouble would follow. Or as political commentators, perhaps they read the political scene more astutely than other people did. Isaiah could see that Syria and Ephraim were feebler than people in Jerusalem hoped or feared.

Yet these prophets themselves often talked as if the process may have been the reverse of this. The background of Amos' ministry was that he had seen nightmare visions such as those related in 7.1–9 and 8.1–3. He 'somehow' knew that the 'Day of Yahweh'[2] was about to happen in Ephraim, and that it was not good news, as the people thought (see 5.18–20). Yahweh had shared this with him. The question he then had to handle was why this was so and what were its implications. Analogously, the beginning of Isaiah's ministry is his nightmare vision of the calamity that Yahweh intends to bring on Judah, and is bringing even now as the Holy One commissions him to stop up people's eyes and ears so that they cannot see or hear (6.1–13). He, too, then has to handle the question why this is so and what are its implications—questions to which chapters 1–5 now give the answers. It is not that the prophets' moral and social critique makes them infer that doom is coming on the people of God. It is their awareness of doom coming on the people that makes them look for the reasons in the people's life.

Politically, too, the prophets' revelations began from their mysterious knowledge of what Yahweh was planning to do. As well as knowing about that eventual calamity, Isaiah also knew that in the shorter term Yahweh was going to see to it that Assyria would defeat Ephraim and Syria, the northern neighbours who were leaning on Judah to ally with them. This had nothing in particular to do with political plausibilities. There is no reason to infer that Isaiah had more human political insight than the kings of Judah, Ephraim, and Syria and their advisers. Isaiah just knew what Yahweh was going to do. And it had nothing to do with what was deserved, though it did have something to do with theology. Judah deserved no deliverance; the certainty of deliverance from Ephraim and Syria derived from the faithfulness of Yahweh. These prophets sensed that calamity was coming first, and asked questions about it afterwards.

These prophets sensed that calamity was coming first, and asked questions about it afterwards

Not the Last Word...

Fortunately for themselves and for us, this last example shows how the prophets had dreams as well as nightmares. The most basic dream is that the decimation of the people through God's punishment, even if it is followed by further trouble for the remains of the 'tree,' is not the last word. 'The holy seed is its stump' (Isa 6.13). Humanly speaking, a tree that has been felled and burned can hardly grow again, but the destiny of God's tree is not limited by regular rules of nature. Similar considerations emerge from Hosea. Hosea and Gomer had a nightmare marriage that ended in divorce. The Torah forbade a divorced couple from marrying each other again (Deut 24.1–4) —we are not sure of the reasons for this. The existence of that prohibition adds force to the fact that Yahweh bids Hosea seek out Gomer once more and re-marry her. It provides a picture of God's dream for Ephraim. Even divorce does not terminate Yahweh's concern for the people and Yahweh's commitment to it. Even while laying down a rule in the Torah about this matter, Yahweh can decide not to abide by the rule.

The prophets were people who looked at the present in the light of the past and in the light of the future, and also looked at the future in the light of the present. They called Israel to live in the present in the light of the future. They knew that God could envisage a nightmare future, but also that God had that dream vision for the future, too. They pictured this dream future in the light of the past—what God had done before gave God and them the ways to picture the future for people. I am struck by the way that every element in Ezekiel's systematic portrayal of God's vision for the people in Ezekiel 34–48 involves nothing more (but nothing less) than a divinely-inspired technicolour reworking of the key promises and key gifts that God had given the people before.

In a sense they had nothing to say that was not implicit in the story of the past

The prophets thus called Israel to live in the light of its own story. All the major elements in the story from creation to the fall of Jerusalem appear somewhere or other in the messages of the prophets. They see the elements in this story as providing clues for understanding God and for understanding God's people in the future. Whatever happened in their communities or was threatened for them, they kept coming back to that story and asking once more what might be its implications. They did not see themselves as great innovators, as people with a novel message. In a sense they had nothing to say that was not implicit in the story of the past. They wanted to remedy people's lack of 'knowledge,' but this 'knowledge' (*da'at*) was not a matter of mental awareness of facts. It was a matter of 'acknowledgment' or recognition of facts that were already before them.

If we live with the aftermath of calamity, they will thrill us with their insight into God's dreams for us

Prophets today will share with us God's nightmares and God's dreams for us. They will frighten us with their insight into the terrible disaster that hangs over the people of God, though if they have to do that, they will also encourage us with God's vision for our escaping disaster or finding new life the other side of disaster. If we live with the aftermath of calamity, like the church in Europe, they will thrill us with their insight into God's dreams for us. But as they do that, their encouragement will come in the context of affirming that the calamity had to be, and was deserved, and needs to be faced.

Question for Reflection

- What are the consequences of avoiding discussing the things we fear are true? Or avoiding talking about dreams and possibilities?

3 Poets and Actors

A prophet speaks like a poet and behaves like an actor.

As God's nightmares and dreams, the prophets' visions demand be taken with absolute seriousness, but not as direct, literal portrayals of reality. Dreams and nightmares are not like that. To put it another way, the prophets were poets. While some parts of their books are prose sermons, for the most part their prophecies take the form of lines of verse, with the features of Hebrew poetry such as parallelism. They are full of imagery and symbolism, of simile and metaphor, of hyperbole and rhetorical question. Commonly they do not describe things directly, in the way that (say) much of the teaching in the Torah does. Characteristically, their words are anything but straightforward (see for example 1 Kgs 13; 22). Receiving a word from a prophet does not suddenly make life less complicated, as if we now know things we did not know before. It is more like listening to one of Jesus' parables.

Receiving a word from a prophet does not suddenly make life less complicated

We should thus expect Christian prophets to speak in pictures, as (in my experience) they commonly do. Often, receiving their revelations from God will leave us initially puzzled rather than quite clear what God is saying to us—as was the case when the disciples heard Jesus' parables. A prophet's picture may well require interpretation.

One reason for this is that deep truths about God cannot be put in straightforward language that speaks only to the rational mind. They require imagery that can reach the whole person. Another is that we do not want to receive God's truth, and God in mercy sometimes avoids speaking to us clearly because that is to put us into a worse position than the one we already occupy. Prophets speak in pictures because we can then avoid seeing what God is saying, yet also because the picture may get underneath our guard and break through our resistance.

Prophets act as well as speak. Sometimes they act in a way that directly implements their message, even though they do not attempt to be social reformers. Like their words, their acts tend to be illustrative of their vision, rather than a down-to-earth exposition of it. So Isaiah goes about naked and barefoot for three years to dramatize what Yahweh intends to bring about (Isa 20), and Jeremiah smashes a pitcher with the same intent (Jer 19). Such acts had various significances. They provided vivid and worrying illustrations of what the words announced. They constituted another way of getting beneath people's guard and breaking through people's resistance, another alternative to straightforward words. Worst of all, they actually put Yahweh's words into effect, in the way that putting a ring on someone's finger contributes to the process of marrying someone, or returning it contributes to a break-up.

Prophets were people with the capacity to be outrageous. This also emerges in another way. In its first usages in the Old Testament, the verb 'prophesy' refers not to speech with identifiable content but to some unusual form of behaviour that suggests that a person is under supernatural influence (see Num 11; 1 Sam 10; 18.10; 19). Prophesying functioned as a sign in the way that tongues sometimes does—perhaps it was something very like tongues. As well as providing individuals with evidence that God was indeed involved with them, prophesying could be the evidence for other people that the person's words should be heeded, but it does not constitute these words. The verb does come to be used as the regular verb to describe the delivering of a verbal message from God, and this comes to be its most frequent usage. But 'prophesying' links with an activity that the NRSV can translate as 'raving' or 'being in a frenzy' (even if these precise translations give a misleading impression). We should not be surprised if prophets fail to observe the usual decorum of suburban congregations in the historic churches.

We should not be surprised if prophets fail to observe the usual decorum of suburban congregations

So prophecy will put before the church a challenge to our will, our imagination, and our insight. Perhaps God sends us prophets because we cannot respond to more straightforward address. And/or perhaps God does not send us too many prophets because we cannot respond to address that is not straightforward.

Questions for Reflection

- What are the advantages of speaking in pictures and metaphors? What problems does this bring, and how can we respond to these?

- How can we create space in our churches to allow God to speak in ways that are not straightforward? Why do we find these ways difficult or challenging?

4 Being Offensive

A prophet is not afraid to be offensive.

Death is no joke. In our culture, the funeral is the one occasion where formality still obtains. In the Old Testament, a death is the one occasion when we find David expressing his feelings, even if someone in his court ghostwrote his lament (2 Sam 1.17–27). On a later occasion Israelites once heard a solemn prophet uttering a funeral dirge. *She has fallen, she will not rise again* (Amos 5.2). Who is this? Who has died? It is Israel itself. *Maiden Israel* turns out to be the subject of the verb. The people who overhear the dirge ask who has died and discover that they have. Yahweh likewise bids Ezekiel, *You, lead a dirge for the leaders of Israel* (Ezek 19.1). Thus Ezekiel intones an allegory about a mother who watches one of her sons being dragged off to Egypt and another one being dragged off to Babylon. The devastating and heartless picture constitutes another attempt to get the city, the leadership, and the exiles to see sense.

There is a place in Moab called Madmen (which would offer temptation to someone prophesying in English) and a place near Jerusalem called Madmenah. Fortunately or unfortunately *madmenah* is also Hebrew for a cesspit. Isaiah thus puns on the name, promising that *the Moabites will be trampled in their place like straw being trampled in a cesspit, and they will spread their hands in the midst of it to swim as swimmers spread their hands to swim, but he will humble their majesty* (Isa 25.10–11). Moabites swimming in a cesspit? Commentators routinely critique or defend or apologize for the image, but ultimately there is nothing more violent here than appears in many other passages in the Old Testament. What is noteworthy is the bad taste, by Western standards—and perhaps by middle-eastern ones, too.

Ezekiel is the master of bad taste

Ezekiel is the master of bad taste—oddly, perhaps, for a priest. One prize instance is his allegory about Jerusalem (Ezek 16) with its portrait of the baby wallowing in blood, then lying naked Lolita-like in puberty, which becomes a lewdly detailed account of her subsequent promiscuity and a faithlessness that involves her paying for sex rather than charging for it.

Yahweh inspires prophets to speak in the manner of late-night satellite television as well as that of the BBC.

Rebuke and Hope

5

A prophet confronts the confident with rebuke and the downcast with hope.

Popular understanding assumes that the importance of the prophets lies in their anticipatory witness to Jesus. They do give such witness, but one can read page after page of the prophets without coming across any statement that directly constitutes witness to Jesus. God summoned and spoke to the prophets so that they could minister directly to the people of their day.

This indeed involved them in promising that one day God would send someone who would fulfil all the hopes attaching to Israel's anointed king, its 'messiah.' But it is striking that they never use the Hebrew word 'messiah' to refer to *the* Messiah. The word 'messiah' comes only twice in the Latter Prophets (Isaiah, Jeremiah, Ezekiel, and the Twelve). Once it is a description of the Persian king Cyrus, who is God's anointed one in bringing down Babylon and opening up the possibility of Judah's restoration (Isa 45.1). In keeping with the common usage in other books, once it refers to Judah's current anointed king (Hab 3.13). Of course, the prophets did speak of a future figure who would fulfil God's promises to David and God's expectations of David (for example Jer 23.5–6) but they never use the word 'messiah' of this person.

They embody God's desire to speak to people about the realities, the temptations, and the pressures of their day

That is a symbol of the fact that they do not speak much of this coming person. Their focus does not lie on that far future. In the exercise of their ministry, they focus on speaking to their own people in the present. They embody God's desire to speak to people about the realities, the temptations, and the pressures of their day. As God's word for us, the way they minister to God's people in their day is at least as significant as the way they talk about the future Messiah.

When they do talk about the future, their direct reason for doing so is to help their own people live in the present. We always need to live in the light of the future. Indeed, we always do live in the light of the future; the question is whether it is an imagined future (feared or hoped for) or a real one.

The two halves of Ezekiel's ministry provide a noteworthy instance. Before the fall of Jerusalem in 587, people think the future will turn out all right, and Ezekiel's impossible task is to convince them that things are going to be much worse than they believe. After the fall of Jerusalem, however, people sink into despair, and Ezekiel's task is to convince them that things are going to be much better than they believe. As a prophet, Ezekiel's task was to confront the confident with bad news and the downcast with hope.

As a prophet, Ezekiel's task was to confront the confident with bad news and the downcast with hope

The same insight emerges from the book of Isaiah as a whole. When people were enthusiastic in their praise, generous in their giving, and fervent in their prayer, Isaiah ben Amoz told them they were a burden that Yahweh wished to cast off because their life outside church did not match their heart-felt worship (Isa 1.10–20). (We are inclined to assume that the problem is that they were not sincere in the sense that their worship was only outward, but this is not Isaiah's critique. There is no reason to think that they did not mean every 'hallelujah'; the problem Isaiah confronts is the mis-match between their life of worship and their life in the world. They worshipped Yahweh with enthusiastic hearts, but their community life was not lived Yahweh's way.) When people despaired of their future because they knew Yahweh had brought calamity upon them, though they did not understand why, Second Isaiah told them that there were grounds for hope. Yahweh is one who knows how to say that enough is enough. When trouble comes, this does not mean that Yahweh has cast us off forever.

If God sends us prophets, we should expect them to confront us in the same way. We do not need prophets to tell us what we already think or to affirm our current feelings.

Prophets may bring good news or bad news, but if it is good news, they are probably not telling the truth. Not for nothing does Ahab call Elijah a troubler of Israel, even if Ahab is himself Israel's real troubler (1 Kgs 18.17–18).

Questions for Reflection

- Which do we find it easier to speak to others—words of rebuke or words of hope? Why is this?
- What might it mean for your church to live in the light of the future?
- How can we better connect our worship and our way of life?

Speaking to the People of God 6

A prophet's task is mostly to speak to the people of God.

Prophets sometimes spoke *to* other nations and often spoke *about* other nations, but they usually spoke *to* the people of God. As the people of God, Israel and Judah were of course themselves nations, but the prophets addressed these nations as entities to which Yahweh was committed and they addressed them concerning their own commitment to Yahweh. Their primary significance for us lies in the way they address the people of God.

It is common to speak of the church having a prophetic ministry to society, but I am not clear that this emerges from the nature of Old Testament prophecy. If we ask after the nature of Israel's vocation in relation to other peoples, it more likely lay in a vocation to be a people that embodied an alternative vision of what it meant to

It is we ourselves who need to heed the prophetic word

be a human community. It is a community with God at its centre that would demonstrate the blessing that comes from having God at the centre. If the church has a ministry to society, it again lies in embodying such an alternative vision. If we care to call that a 'prophetic' ministry, we may do so. But in the absence of our *embodying* such an alternative vision, the attempt to exercise a prophetic ministry by the use of prophetic *words* is surely unlikely to have much effect. It is we ourselves who need to heed the prophetic word so that we may become the alternative community. Prophets are people who call the church to be the people of God instead of being an imitation of the world.

Similarly, it has been common to think of the prophets as social reformers, but I have noted that it is not clear that they were that. A social reformer is someone with a vision for society and some ideas about how to implement that vision—some practical policies that the reformer urges the community to adopt. Some of the prophets were indeed people who had a vision for society, though this applies in particular to prophets such as Amos and Micah; it is not a central characteristic of prophets in general. But even in the case of these prophets, their vocation was not the developing of practical plans for reform. They were usually quite general in their social vision, and when they were being specific and concrete, it was usually in critique, not in formulating positive proposals. They critiqued legal procedures that worked for people who were rich and/or powerful and worked against ordinary people (for example Amos 2.6–8), but they did not outline proposals for judicial reform to put this matter right. There were people in Israel who accepted that vocation and sought to think of ways to turn the prophets' visions into practical proposals that they could urge on the community, but they were not the prophets. They were the anonymous figures whose God-inspired work came to be incorporated in the teaching in the Torah, such as the 'Deuteronomists.' It is these figures who were Israel's social reformers.

Yahweh's summons to the prophets was to focus on Yahweh's vision for the society as the people of God. They were to find ways of reminding people of the nature of God as the compassionate and powerful one, the committed and decisive one, the fair and just one, the faithful and authoritative one. They were to find ways of reminding the people of their vocation to image this God so that the life of the people of God spoke to the world. And they were to find ways of bringing home to the people of God the terrible cost of failing to do that. They were to draw them to turn away from wrongdoing and from other religious commitments, and to turn to Yahweh.

Prophets today will then exercise their ministry to the church. It may be that they will need to speak about God's expectations of the wider society or of the nations, but there is then a trap of which they will need to be aware. It is possible to fulminate about society or about the nations in such a way as to make the church feel reassured and self-righteous. This is not the implication of the way the Old Testament prophets spoke of and to the nations. Indeed, the story of Jonah warns against that trap. There it is the foreign nation that knows instinctively how to respond to a prophet. The prophets would have given their eye-teeth for a response from the people of God like the one Nineveh gave. The people of God have no room for self-righteousness over against the nations.

When prophets said that God intended to put the nations down, sometimes their aim was to deliver the people of God from a false alliance with and reliance on the nations. A modern analogy for this alliance might be the close association between church and nation in Europe and the USA. Despite the formal dissociation of church and state in the USA, there, as in Europe, the church's sharing the gospel with other peoples has been systematically interwoven with the nation's winning an empire. Prophets will perceive this alliance and warn the church about it.

Sometimes the prophets spoke of the destiny of the nations because the nations were a threat to the people of God. There are many countries in which this is so today. Prophets will promise the people of God that the threat will not last forever.

A prophet is someone independent of the institutional pressures of church and state.

In David's lifetime, the most prominent prophet was Nathan, and in effect he was on the king's staff. So perhaps was Gad, the only other prophet who is mentioned in David's story. This makes it easy for Nathan to be the king's yes-man (2 Sam 7.1–3). It also gives him opportunity to confront David (2 Sam 12), but one wonders whether a little more confrontation might have been appropriate throughout the story in 2 Samuel 13–1 Kings 2. Subsequently a king such as Ahab has hundreds of prophetic advisers who can be relied on to be yes-men (1 Kgs 22), as the kings of other nations had many supportive prophets.

When Amos goes around Bethel speaking of disaster to come on the nation, Amaziah, the senior pastor at Bethel, urges him to desist. He should go back to Judah and earn his living prophesying there. Judah will, of course, welcome words about disaster for the northern kingdom. In reply, Amos suggests that Amaziah has misunderstood Amos's position. He is not a prophet like Gad and Nathan who is in the king's employ and can be sent about by a royal official such as Amaziah. Nor is he a trained prophet like the people who belonged to Elijah's prophetic seminary. 'I am no prophet, nor a prophet's son,' he says. Admittedly the NRSV may be wrong in rendering Amos' response in the present tense. The Hebrew sentence is a noun clause, literally 'I no prophet...' One has to infer from the context whether such a statement refers to past, present, or future, and NIV renders it as past—which fits Amos' subsequent past-tense testimony about Yahweh's taking him and

The fact that they 'see' supernaturally and accurately does not guarantee that they serve Yahweh

sending him to prophesy. But the main point is little affected by this uncertainty. Either way, there are prophets who work for the king and prophets who have been trained in prophetic seminaries, and Amos distances himself from such prophets. It is thus ironic that the word Amos raises questions about, the word *nabi'*, eventually becomes *the* positive word for a prophet. The word that Amaziah himself uses to describe Amos is 'seer,' so evidently seers, too, can be in the service of the government (2 Sam 24:11) and could be driven into compromise and thus be rejected by Yahweh (see Micah 3:7). The fact that they 'see' supernaturally and accurately does not guarantee that they serve Yahweh.

Prophets on the Payroll?

Evidently there is an 'office' of prophet, occupied by people such as Nathan and presupposed by someone such as Amaziah, but this office is not occupied by prophets such as Elijah and Elisha or Amos and Jeremiah. They are not on the payroll of the people of God, like priests. Who was king in Judah, and who were priests, was fixed. God had taken an initiative long ago with regard to kings and priests, in line with the instincts of Israel itself ('make us a king like the nations'). After that, normally God let things work themselves out in accordance with the rules of descent. With prophets, however, God can take an initiative and intervene. There is no parallel set of human expectations to observe or break. Thus Israel knew no women priests and few women political leaders, but it did have women prophets. And in contexts of church renewal and revival God has often used women prophets (whether or not they were called such) in churches that would not recognize women priests or pastors.

There is nothing wrong with being on the payroll—Paul argued that it was fine for a servant of Christ to be supported financially by the community. But if you are on the payroll, it is much harder for you to take a 'prophetic' stance in relation to that community. You cannot bark at the hand that feeds you without risking its cutting off your food supply, and you may have other mouths to feed as well as your own. Your experience and that of your family may correspond to that of Micaiah, who finds himself on a diet of bread and water for bringing God's word to his people (1 Kgs 22).

To put it in modern terms, it is virtually impossible for a pastor to be a prophet

To put it in modern terms, it is virtually impossible for a pastor to be a prophet. In this context, by a pastor I mean a professional, a person who receives a salary from the people whom he or she pastors, and I speak of this professional pastor's ministry to this congregation that pays this salary. It is possible for a prophet to be a pastor—Gerhard von Rad described Ezekiel thus,[3] and I would do the same of Second Isaiah. But they were on no one's payroll, as far as we know—Ezekiel would have been a priest if he had not been exiled, but there was no temple to be looked after in Babylon. There is a sad irony here that I press on ordinands, and they do not thank me for it. Many men and women go to theological college to train for the church's ministry because they have already exercised a significant informal ministry in church or para-church contexts. They have been prophetic-type figures, one might say. Their faithfulness and fruitfulness in such contexts encourages people to point them towards more formal ministry, but they then have to face the fact that they surrender the capacity to be prophetic once they are ordained and are on the church's payroll.

When we are pastoring individuals, it is necessary for us to be prophetic. It is therefore to be hoped that being prophetic is possible as well as necessary. This seems to have been so in Israel. The psalms imply that there were people—presumably Levites and priests—who acted as prophetic pastors who brought the word of God to people when they came to pour out their hurt and anger to God (compare the story of Hannah and Eli in 1 Sam 1). In this sense, a pastor who is not a prophet is not a pastor either. And in saying that a pastor cannot be a prophet, perhaps more generally I exaggerate the point, like a prophet. Perhaps one might rather say that monumental pressures not to be prophetic come upon a person who is on the church's payroll. If I am a professional pastor, the only safe stance is thus to assume that I cannot now be prophetic. I must therefore encourage the prophetic ministry of other people who are not on the payroll, who may be able to say the confrontational things that I cannot say—not least, encourage the prophetic ministry of people who may be able to say them to me.

Drawn into the Company of Heaven

Prophets are people who are surprised to find themselves in the role they have. You do not seek or volunteer or pray to be a prophet. Even Isaiah proves the rule. He indeed volunteers, but he does so in the context of finding that God has already drawn him into the company of heaven, where God is looking for someone to send. Being a prophet means finding yourself drawn into that company and compelled to speak for God. This experience may well contradict your life experience so far, as was the case with Amos, and you may well seek to resist the pressure, as Jeremiah did, or you may not be able to see how you *Prophets are people who are surprised to find themselves in the role they have* can fulfil such a calling successfully, as Second Isaiah did. I once heard the Principal of a rabbinic seminary commenting that when someone told him that they felt called to be a rabbi, he was inclined to send them to a psychiatrist. It is mad to want to be a prophet. Jeremiah commented on how easy it is to deceive oneself into believing that we have a message from God for people (Jer 23.25–26).

A prophet models a kind of relationship with God that is God's intention for everyone. Moses eventually found the pressure of the people to be too much, and told God he could carry on no longer (Num 11.14). Yahweh's spirit came on seventy senior members of the community, apparently as a sign that the people are to take them as seriously as they take Moses (!). But two of the senior members who stayed in the camp continued to 'prophesy.' Joshua bade Moses stop them, but Moses was unfazed by what had happened. He did not feel the need to control what Yahweh's spirit might do: 'Would that all Yahweh's people were prophets, and that Yahweh would put his spirit on them.'

It is intrinsic to the nature of prophecy that it is not under the control of the leaders of the community. In principle anyone may prophesy. That principle is restated in Joel 2.28–29, which makes explicit that in due course Yahweh's spirit will be poured out on people of both sexes, young and old, slaves as well as masters. Acts 2 saw this happening at Pentecost, but it has not usually characterized the church. Yet the promise suggests that it is always God's will for us, and it invites us to look for its fulfilment.

In our own context we might need to ask who would be the kind of people that we would *not* expect to be prophets. These are the people God is likely to want to use as prophets.

Questions for Reflection

- Are there ways in which we can build the role of prophets into our churches without threatening the compromise that can arise from them being on the payroll?

- In what practical ways can we enable the prophetic and the pastoral to work together?

- What do we need to do to be open to the prophetic ways God is at work in our own lives—how can we learn to hear the prophetic word of God for ourselves?

Scary Person, Scary God

8

A prophet is a scary person who mediates the activity of a scary God.

One of the expressions that the Books of Kings use to describe prophets is the phrase 'man of God.' In modern parlance 'man of God' (or 'woman of God') suggests someone of deep spirituality, of committed prayer life, of spiritual insight. And no doubt prophets were such people. But this is not the connotation of the term 'man of God' in the Old Testament. The phrase especially suggests a somewhat austere and frightening figure with mysterious powers. A man of God is someone who utters words of fearful significance that can be followed by signs that can be both destructive and constructive (see the stories in 1 Kgs 13; 2 Kgs 1; 2 Kgs 4–8; 2 Kgs 13.14–19).

A man of God is someone who utters words of fearful significance

Prophets are such figures because they reflect and mediate the nature of their God. Yahweh is somewhat mysterious, unpredictable, and frightening as well as consistent, reassuring, and encouraging. The man after God's heart who experienced God being full of grace and commitment through the prophet Nathan's ministry in 2 Samuel 7 also experienced God offering the choice of famine, defeat, or plague through the prophet Gad in 2 Samuel 24 (see also the story in 2 Sam 6). The toughness of God and prophet in these stories reminds us of the toughness of Peter and of Peter's God in Acts 5.

We should expect prophetic ministry today to reduce the domestication of God that characterises us

If prophetic ministry is exercised today, then, we should expect this to reduce the domestication of God that characterizes us as evangelicals and charismatics.

One of the reasons why the God of the Old Testament prophets is scary is that they have no one else on whom to project scary aspects of supernatural reality. Christian faith has usually been inclined to various forms of dualism, and the prophets would stand against that. We project the scary onto Satan. The prophets were insistently convinced that Yahweh was the only god who really deserved to be called God, and they denied Israel the right to treat other heavenly beings as if they had any power. Further, whereas the nations around them might assume that there were many demons that could affect the lives of people, the prophets never spoke in these terms.

We might therefore expect prophets today once again to stand against Christian inclination to think that there are demonic powers that are powerful enough to oppress people and frustrate God's purpose. They will remind us that there is only one God, only one being who has real power in heaven and on earth. If the God of love is also a scary God, at least there is no doubt that this God is in control.

Questions for Reflection

- When have you received or needed to give a word from God that was scary? How did you know it was of God?

- Do you find it easy to believe that God is the source of all power, even when that power is used in frightening ways?

Boldness and Freedom 9

A prophet intercedes with boldness and praises with freedom.

Prophets are mediators between God and humanity, and they mediate in both directions. We usually think of them as people who especially bring God's word to us, but they also bring our words to God. Both capacities emerge from their membership of Yahweh's cabinet. Their listening to its deliberations enables them to share the results of these with the human beings who will be affected by them. It also gives them the opportunity to take part in these deliberations in order to persuade the cabinet to come to a different decision, and this is what we see in the stories of people such as Amos (7.1–8.3). Both activities, the preaching and the prayer, have the same aim, to make it possible for Yahweh's positive purpose to be fulfilled and for Yahweh's threats to be abandoned.

The story of Jonah illustrates especially vividly one key way in which a prophet gets Yahweh's threat of punishment averted. His task is to declare that trouble is coming on Nineveh, this causes Nineveh to turn from its wrongdoing, and then Yahweh's threat can be withdrawn. Jeremiah 18 states the principle that underlies this story. It also states a correlative principle, that seeing Yahweh's promises fulfilled depends on a life of right-doing. A prophet urges people on in right-doing, in order that they may see Yahweh's promises fulfilled.

Praying equally emerges from that membership of God's cabinet

But preaching is not enough for a prophet. It is accompanied by praying, and this must be so, because praying equally emerges from that membership of God's cabinet. A person who hears that there is trouble coming on people can hardly simply accept this. Such a person would *have* to beseech Yahweh to have mercy. At least, this is the instinct of a prophet such as Amos, though the problem with Jonah is of course that he did not want to be the means of wrongdoers being forgiven. It is as an intercessor that Abraham is called a prophet, on the very first occasion that the word 'prophet' comes in the Bible (Gen 20.7). Prophets are mediators between heaven and earth. They bring human beings a word from God that they could not have attained by ordinary means, and they also take words from human beings to God that would not otherwise reach God.

Of course there is no guarantee that Yahweh will acquiesce with the urgings of a prophet, as Amos also makes clear. Yahweh accepts Amos's first two prayers, but refuses his second two. There are times when God says 'Enough' and refuses to relent. Jeremiah and Hosea had the same experience (see Jer 14–15; Hos 5.15–6.1–6). On the other hand, it may be that even then a prophet does not too soon take 'No' for an answer. The prophet's challenge is still to get God to have a change of mind, in keeping with the occasions when God does that in Scripture. The prayers of a prophet correspond to one of the three main ways of speaking to God that appear in the psalms, the laments, which cover what we call supplication (for ourselves) and intercession (for others). They ask God to do what God is not inclined to do, and resist pressure to take no for an answer.

Prophetic Praise

Praying in the manner of a lament is not the only way in which a prophet speaks to God on behalf of the people. The Psalms' other two main ways of speaking to God are two forms of praise, hymns and thanksgivings. Hymns praise God for who God always is and for God's great acts of salvation. Thanksgivings give testimony to what God has just done for me or for us. After Abraham, Scripture's second prophet is Miriam, and the way in which she acts as a prophet is in joining Moses in leading people in praise and dancing after the deliverance at the Red Sea (Exod 15.20–21). The greatest of the judges, Deborah, is also a prophet, and in an analogous way she takes the lead over Barak in praise for what Yahweh has done in delivering the people, as she does in making that victory happen (Jdg 4–5). Then the opening of the story of the monarchy includes the thanksgiving of Hannah, who praises God like a prophet as she speaks of what Yahweh is doing, and as she speaks of Yahweh's 'anointed,' the king whom her son will anoint (indeed, two of them).

If there are prophets in our midst, they will give themselves in prayer urging God not to bring calamity on the church. They will pray not once but twice, as often as they have a sense that God plans trouble for the church, until God forbids them to pray. Even then they may wonder whether God is merely testing them, and they may not give up. They will lead us in praise and dance that speak powerfully of the nature of God as the church's powerful and generous king and deliverer, and celebrate the great things God has done for us and the great things God still intends.

- How does the connection between prophecy and prayer challenge some understandings of what it means to be prophetic?
- In what ways is the praise in your church prophetic?

Personality and Culture 10

A prophet ministers in a way that reflects his or her personality and time.

There is a paradox about prophecy. Of all inspired Scripture, along with the revelation to Moses it is prophecy that is described most transcendently as words that come direct from God. Prophets receive God's dictation—they hear God speak and pass on God's actual words (for example Ezek 17.1–21). Or God's words are put in their mouth (for example Isa 51.16). Or God speaks 'by means of them'—literally, speaks 'by their hand' (for example Jer 37.2); their tongues are like the musical instrument that God plays.

The paradox is that the individual humanness of the prophets also comes out in their prophecy. There is little mistaking the words of Jeremiah for those of Isaiah, or the words of Ezekiel for those of Second Isaiah. *How* they speak and *what* they say reflects who they are. God uses them as the people they are to bring the message they can bring.

When we hear an alleged prophetic message today, if we know the person we may be tempted to comment, 'That's just what I would have expected *him* or *her* to say.' We may be right that they say what we might have been able to envisage them saying, but in itself this does not raise questions about whether God was speaking through them. Prophecy comes through the human personality. It does not bypass that personality.

Prophecy comes through the human personality

Individuals and Community

There is another, related paradox about prophecy. Because Western culture has put a high value on the individual, it has appreciated the prophets because they could seem to stand like lone individuals. They could seem to have realized their own distinctive individuality in a remarkable way. Yet this likely exaggerates and/or misinterprets their individuality. The Books of Kings speak much of those prophetic seminaries or prophetic communities referred to above. Here prophets apparently learned and ministered together, like (for instance) the groups of prophets protected by Obadiah

(1 Kgs 18). Nor was it only these early prophets who worked in the midst of communities. Isaiah had a group of disciples whom he could commission to treasure his teaching (Isa 8.16). If Jeremiah was alone, he saw this as a regrettable disadvantage of his particular prophetic vocation, not as the logical fulfilment of any prophetic vocation; and even he had Baruch. Prophecy is naturally exercised in the midst of a prophetic community. Here (one might hypothesize) prophets could test out messages that might be the word of Yahweh, before declaring them to their intended audience. Here they could find encouragement to speak out, and find support when they paid the price for their ministry. Sometimes they had to take a lone stand, but that was not their aim. It was not of the essence of their ministry. Most of them lived and worked in association with others. For contemporary prophets, too, that will be for their encouragement and the protection—and for that of the wider community of faith to which they belong and in which they minister.

Questions for Reflection

- Do you normally expect prophetic insights to reflect the culture in which they are expressed or to transcend that culture?
- What does the communal nature of prophecy suggest regarding the issue of independence and accountability?

Success and Failure

11

A prophet is likely to fail.

Prophets are not infallible. They make mistakes. Three notable mistake-makers are Elijah, Hananiah, and Jeremiah. Elijah makes one mistake, and Yahweh meets him where he is and coaxes him back (1 Kgs 19). As far as we can tell from the Book of Jeremiah, Hananiah's whole prophetic ministry was a mistake. Everything he said was scriptural, but he did not know what time it was. He was preaching from the wrong texts in the wrong century. Intending to be scriptural does not mean that you are actually being scriptural. Jeremiah himself went though a number of crises in his relationship with God, and found himself rebuked and offered restoration on at least one spectacular occasion (see Jer 15). If we exercise a prophetic ministry, we need to be wary of thinking that we have become infallible.

There is another sense in which prophets fail. They may make no mistakes, but they are unlikely to succeed in achieving the aim that God set before them. In this sense, by and large the great prophets all seem to have been failures. Amos and Hosea failed to halt the slide of Ephraim that hit the bottom with the fall of Samaria. Isaiah and Micah failed to halt the slide of Judah that reached new depths of apostasy in the time of Manasseh. Huldah and Jeremiah failed to halt the further slide that led to the fall of Jerusalem. Ezekiel and Second Isaiah failed to get the exilic community to look at its situation through Yahweh's eyes and to hope and prepare for the restoration of the community. Perhaps Third Isaiah, Haggai, Zechariah, and Malachi were the nearest to being successes, as the Second Temple community does seem to have learned to live with the Torah written into its heart to a much greater extent than the First Temple community. (Ironically, the very greatest of the prophetic successes was Jonah, but he only succeeded with foreigners, and only in a parable!)

Being six years out of Britain, I do not think I have a specific word for the British church. But if I were a prophet where I now live in Southern California, I would declare that the church here is on the way to the same experience as overcame the church in the Eastern Mediterranean in the first millennium and the church in Europe in the second millennium. As the heartland of the gospel moved from the Eastern Mediterranean to Europe and then from

Europe to the USA, so it has now moved from the USA to the two-thirds world, to Latin America, Africa, and Asia. As the church in the Eastern Mediterranean all but died in the first millennium and the church in Europe all but died in the second millennium, so the church in the USA is dying. One way to express the inevitability of its death in Southern California is to note how comprehensively it falls into one or other of two misunderstandings of worship. Either its worship is 'moralistic, didactic, and instructive' or it is 'excessively therapeutic and narcissistic.' Both didactic and therapeutic tendencies are inclined 'to talk about meeting with God, rather than to enact such a meeting with the one who is profoundly holy and yet genuinely present.'[4]

Whether I am a prophet or not, I do declare this, though I do not expect to be heeded. Indeed, it may be that I am wrong, and that God has already abandoned the church here, as God abandoned Jerusalem in Ezekiel's day (see Ezek 9–10). All that is to follow is the formal fall of the city. In Californian culture, one of the ways of denying that death is a reality is by applying vast technological resources to keeping people's bodies alive for as long as possible when the time to die has come. The culture likes to pretend that 'death is optional.'[5] In a parallel way, pastors spend their energy helping their churches deny that God has left them and that death is imminent. As a prophet, I would say this, but I would fail to halt this slide.

The Point of Prophecy

If I were a prophet, then, what would be the point of the declaring? If prophets (nearly) always fail, what is the point of prophecy?

First, the phenomenon of prophecy indicates that God stays ever hopeful of a response from the people. God did not cast off Israel and has not cast off the church—even if God did cast off whole generations or parts of Israel, as God has cast off whole generations or parts of the church. God kept speaking to it, ever hopeful that *this time* there might be a response. The fact that Israel and the church have never heeded prophets in the past does not close off the possibility that *this time* things might be different. Second, the phenomenon of prophecy has been far more important for other people in other times than for the people whom the prophecy directly addressed. Only a few Judeans heard the words of First Isaiah or Second Isaiah or Third Isaiah. Of the people who did hear these words, many fewer heeded. But since their day, countless millions have heard them, and some have heeded them. When the church in Southern California has died, it is possible that the church in the two-thirds world might be able to learn from

> *God stays ever hopeful of a response from the people*

its story. A prophetic word that announced the event might enable that church to reflect on the equivalent perils that might lead to its downfall in the fourth millennium.

With failure usually goes suffering. Prophets not only tend to fail to persuade their people to believe in them. The people of God tend to persecute them for bringing their offensive message (see Matt 5.12). This pattern appears particularly clearly in Jeremiah and in Isaiah 40–55. Solemnly, Second Isaiah tells us of realizing that the persecution that comes from the people of God (perhaps from the Babylonians, too) actually becomes God's means of ministering to them. The vision of the ultimate servant's ministry in Isaiah 52.13–53.12 reflects the prophet's own experience of being misunderstood, devalued, and persecuted. Evidently the prophet had come to see that God could use a prophet's identification with people in their suffering for their sins and willingness to suffer even though one had done nothing to deserve it. It could bring people to their senses and enable them to perceive that they had been seeing things wrong. In accepting this suffering, one could even turn it into an offering to God that could compensate for the failures of one's people and help to put things right with God.

The persecution that comes from the people of God actually becomes God's means of ministering to them

Servant Ministry

While Jesus is the person who supremely fulfils this vision, the New Testament also treats Isaiah 53 as a pattern by which all followers of Jesus will live (see for example Phil 2; 1 Peter 2). Prophets will especially live by it. The very factors that cause God to send prophets, such as people's resistance to listening to God's word by more regular ways such as the exposition of Scripture, are also the factors that are likely to mean that prophets get rejected and persecuted. Like Second Isaiah and the servant in Isaiah 53, they will therefore have the opportunity to make their handling of that experience a means of God's reaching their people through their lives and through their silence, when they have not been able to reach them with their words. And they will have the opportunity to make their accepting of rejection and persecution an offering to God that helps to compensate for their people's resistance to God (compare Col 1.24).

Only a fool would want to be a prophet. A wise person would run away from God's summons, as Jonah did. But the person who fails to escape becomes a blessing and finds great fruitfulness.

Notes

1 See *Philosophical Investigations—Philosophische Untersuchungen* (Oxford: Blackwell/New York: Macmillan, 1953) ¶¶ 65–67.

2 'Yahweh' is God's personal name, as it was revealed to the Israelites. Most English translations replace it with the phrase 'the LORD.'

3 See *Old Testament Theology* Vol 2 (ET Edinburgh: Oliver and Boyd/New York: Harper, 1965) pp 231–32.

4 Walter Brueggemann, 'The Book of Exodus,' in *The New Interpreter's Bible*, Vol 1 (Nashville: Abingdon, 1994) pp 675–981 (see 908).

5 Jane Walmsley, *Brit-Think, Ameri-Think* (reprinted New York: Penguin, 1987) p 126.